First edition for North America published by Barron's Educational Series, Inc., 1999.

English translation Copyright © 1999 by Barron's Educational Series, Inc.

Copyright © 1996 Éditions Nathan, Paris, France
Original edition: *Petit Mega Autour du Monde*

All inquiries should be addressed to:
Barron's Educational Series, Inc.
250 Wireless Boulevard
Hauppauge, New York 11788
http://www.barronseduc.com

Library of Congress Catalog Card No. 99-19872
International Standard Book No. 0-7641-5189-4

Library of Congress Cataloging-in-Publication Data

Jugla, Cécile.
  [Petit mega autour du monde. English]
  Children / by Cécile Jugla; illustrated by Isabelle Calin . . . [et al.]. — 1st ed.
    p.   cm. — (Around the world)
  Summary: Depicts children around the world engaged in various activities,
including fishing in the Chinese countryside, reindeer races in Lapland,
and a town feast in Africa.
    ISBN 0-7641-5189-4
    1. Children Cross-cultural studies Juvenile literature.
  [1. Manners and customs.] I. Calin, Isabelle, ill. II. Title.
  III. Series: Around the world
  HQ781.J7913 1999
  305.23—dc21   99-19872
                                                                    CIP

Printed in Hong Kong
987654321

Around the World:

CHILDREN

by Cécile Jugla

Pages 64–79 illustrated by Isabelle Calin
Pages 24–27, 42–43, 54–55, 58–61 illustrated by Emmanuelle Étienne
Pages 30–35, 38–41, 44–45, 50–53, 56–57 illustrated by Jean-Marc Pariselle
Pages 82–89 illustrated by Valérie Stetten
Pages 36–37, 48–49 illustrated by Serge Strosberg
Pages 12–23 illustrated by Marcelino Truong
Sidebars illustrated by Monique Gauriau
Maps by Phillipe Mignon

CONTENTS

WITH THE CHILDREN OF THE WHOLE WORLD

The Americas

The world is sorted
into five big parts
called continents.
They are Asia, Europe,
the Americas, Africa, and Oceania.
You are about to take a trip!
Many children will be your guides.
Some of them will be Yanni, Stewart,
Achouna, Ahmed, Yassama, Kosuke,
Tchen, Jeannette.
They will show you how
they live. You will also
see where they live
and how they play.

Europe

Asia

Africa

Oceania

ASIA

Asia has the most people. Walk with Lakhmi among the crowds of an Indian city. Have fun running in the great desert prairie with Beila. Learn all the secrets of growing rice...

...Also meet

Kosuke

Marouan

Tchen

TURKEY

LEBANON
SYRIA

JORDAN

IRAQ

RED SEA

SAUDI ARABIA

YEMEN

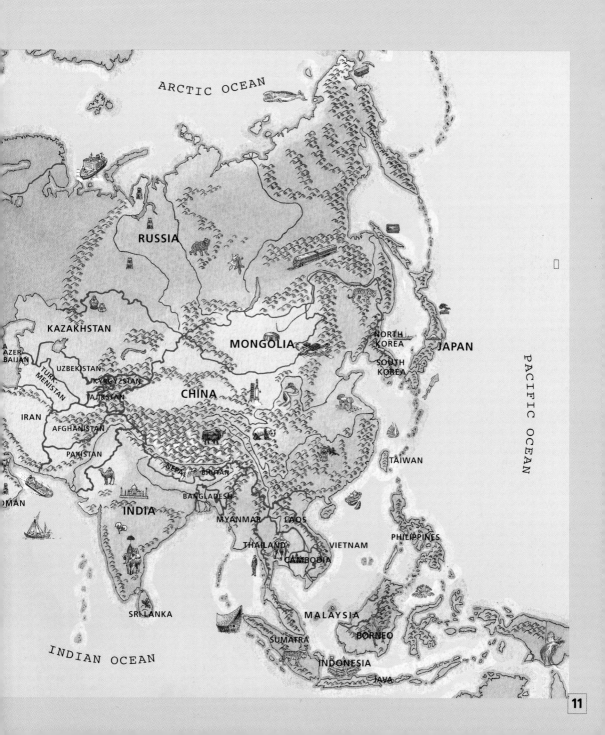

ARCTIC OCEAN

RUSSIA

KAZAKHSTAN

MONGOLIA

NORTH
KOREA

JAPAN

SOUTH
KOREA

AZER-
BAIJAN

UZBEKISTAN

TURK-
MENISTAN

KYRGYZSTAN

TAJIKSTAN

CHINA

IRAN

AFGHANISTAN

PAKISTAN

NEPAL

BHUTAN

TAIWAN

BANGLADESH

OMAN

INDIA

MYANMAR

LAOS

THAILAND

VIETNAM

PHILIPPINES

CAMBODIA

SRI LANKA

MALAYSIA

BORNEO

SUMATRA

INDONESIA

JAVA

INDIAN OCEAN

PACIFIC OCEAN

11

A MIDDLE EASTERN OASIS

Dates are the fruits that grow on palm trees: they grow in bunches like grapes.

To gather them, men climb up the tree trunk. They use a rope to help them climb.

Sun-dried dates are delicious. They are often used in cooking.

An oasis is in the middle of the desert. There is water deep in the ground. This helps fruits and vegetables to grow. They grow in the shade of the trees.

A MIDDLE EASTERN TOWN

Take a big, brightly colored bus to town. There are a lot of things happening. There are a lot of cars. They never stop honking their horns.

Outside of the restaurants, men smoke water pipes called narghiles.

Some women wear veils to hide their faces.

The Bedouins are desert nomads. They wear a scarf on their head. It is a kaffiyeh.

AN INDIAN TOWN

Women wear long pieces of cloth around their bodies. It's called a sari.

Men often wear long white shirts with no collar. The shirts are called kurtas.

This woman has a red dot on her forehead. It means that she is married.

The little girl dressed in blue is Lakhmi. She lives in a very large Indian city. Like most Indians she likes to go to the movies. Her mom is taking her to see a movie. They might see the one advertised on the billboard.

Lakhmi is a little hungry. Her mom buys her a chapati (a flat wheat bread). They will take a rickshaw to the movies. A rickshaw is a cart pulled by a bicycle.

Would you like to taste a chapati? An adult can help you make them with these instructions.

Mix
2 cups of
whole wheat flour
2 cups of white flour
two yogurts

half a stick of butter and a pinch of salt

Knead it all together with your fingers to obtain a smooth dough, divide the dough into 20 little balls and flatten them out with a pastry roller, then ask an adult to cook the chapatis in a frying pan, like pancakes.

THE RICE PADDY

In Asia there are different ways of cooking rice. In China, for example, people eat a delicious Cantonese rice.

Make Cantonese rice with an adult.

cook 1 cup of white rice, prepare an omelette with two eggs and cut it in strips, cut two slices of ham in pieces, and cook 1/2 onion, sliced;

finally put all the ingredients in a pan, add butter, salt, and pepper, and heat it up.

Rice needs a lot of water to grow. That's why the rice paddy is flooded. Before planting the seeds, the ground must be tilled. A buffalo pulls a plow to till the ground.

The rice has grown. Young shoots are replanted in another field.

When the rice is ripe the paddy is dried out. The tops of the plants are brought to the town in batches.

The plants are banged against a large stone roller. This separates the rice grains from the plants.

The rice grains are sun-dried and turned regularly.

Then the rice grain is tossed in large trays. This separates the rice grain from its skin.

Rice is grown for its grain. But the stalks are also very useful. By weaving them you can make

a hat

a basket

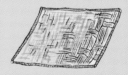

a mat

17

A JAPANESE CITY

To go to school, Kosuke takes the subway. On the subway platform, there are "pushers." They have to push the people to fit inside the train.

In Kosuke's city, there is no unused space. Even the rooftops are used for tennis courts or miniature golf.

Kosuke lives in a very modern city. The streets are crowded with people and cars. Streets have no names. When you invite people to your house you must give them a map. Otherwise they will get lost.

There are 37 children in Kosuke's class. When they're not doing schoolwork, the children have other jobs. They take turns cleaning the classroom and watering the plants...

There is no cafeteria. So the students eat lunch in the classroom.

After school, Kosuke goes to his Kendo class. It's a martial arts class.

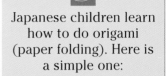

Japanese children learn how to do origami (paper folding). Here is a simple one:

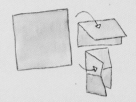

Take a square sheet of paper. Fold it in two in both directions. Open it again and fold

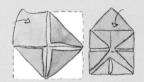

the four corners toward the middle. Turn the square over. Once again, fold the four corners toward the middle.

Put your fingers into the four pockets and close the face. Draw eyes and a mustache. Have fun with your finger puppet.

A JAPANESE FAMILY

Everyone kneels on cushions around a low table to eat.

They eat these foods with chop sticks:

Raw fish dipped in soy sauces

Tofu

White rice

They drink tea in little cups.

The day is over. Kosuke's whole family is home. His mother puts on a silk dress called a kimono. His older sister is taking care of a bonsai (a dwarf tree). Kosuke unfolds his futon, a very hard mattress. This is where he will sleep. Good night!

It's spring. The cherry blossom festival lasts for a week. Kosuke and his family picnic in the park. There they can enjoy the cherry blossoms.

The boys' festival is on May 5. Kosuke flies a kite. It is shaped like a very strong and courageous fish — the carp.

Make a kite in the shape of a fish.

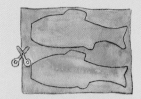

Get tissue paper. Cut out two fish shapes that are alike. Decorate them.

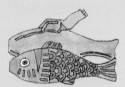

Glue together the outside edges of your fish.

Staple a strip of bendable cardboard around the mouth of the fish.

Attach a kite string and have fun flying it!

A CHINESE CITY

In China, you can do all kinds of things on the street.

Go to the doctor

See a group of people doing Tai'chi chuan (a special exercise)

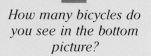

How many bicycles do you see in the bottom picture?

Tchen lives with his parents on a houseboat. It's called a sampan. He has no brothers or sisters. There are too many people in China. So families are only supposed to have one child.

Tchen takes a walk in town with his father. There are a lot of things to see. But Tchen likes to look at the birds in their cages.

For New Year's the family has a big meal that includes

shark fin soup

nems, little pies of soy sauce and meat

glazed duck

Cantonese rice

nougats covered with sesame seeds

For New Year's, Tchen and his family walk in the street. They follow the dragon that chases away bad luck. Firecrackers explode and everyone laughs and has fun!

THE CHINESE COUNTRYSIDE

Chinese children start school when they are seven years old. They learn many things. How to add with an abacus. How to write Chinese characters with a brush and ink.

They also spend a lot of time gardening. And they work in factories. Girls learn to sew and embroider to make their beautiful costumes!

Tchen's cousin is ready for the flower festival. She puts on her embroidered costume and her woolen cap. She hopes to find a husband. In three days, she will give her scarf to the boy she likes. If he wants to marry her, he will keep the scarf.

FISHING WITH A SEAGULL

An oil lamp is at the back of the boat. Its light attracts the fish.

The seagull dives into the water and grabs a fish. It brings the fish back up.

The bird has a ring around its neck. This stops it from

swallowing the fish. The fisherman takes the big fish. He gives a little one to the seagull as a reward.

Tchen's uncle is a fisherman. At night, he goes fishing. He takes a seagull to help him. They go in a strange boat made out of 5 pieces of bamboo.

MONGOLIA

Beila's family lives in Mongolia. Here they raise horses, cows, and sheep.

The men take care of the horses, which walk freely. An urgha is a strange lasso attached to a pole. The men use urghas to catch wild horses. Then they train the horses so they can ride them.

In the morning, the women take the sheep to the prairie. Then they milk the cows and make butter and cheese.

Beila is only six years old. But he is already a good rider. He likes to gallop in the great prairie. This prairie is called a steppe. When he is nine, he will leave his family. He will live at the school in the closest town.

The whole family (children, parents, and grandparents) lives in the yurt. It is a felt tent that is well lit and heated.

Inside it is as comfortable as a house. There is a stove in which dried cow dung is burned. There is also a place to put away clothes and dishes.

Mongols are nomads. This means that they move a lot. When the cows run out of food, the family must move. The grandfather decides where the family will go.

In the winter, the whole family gathers in the yurt. They keep warm around the stove. They also drink a special tea. It is made with salt and butter. The butter has a very strong smell.

EUROPE

Europe is a small continent with
many countries. Each country
has its own customs, festivals,
and traditions. Come with us.
Learn how to dance the flamenco
with Carmen, the Spanish girl. Participate
in the Saint Lucia festival in Sweden.
Race with
reindeer in
Lapland.

ATLANTIC OCEAN

ICE

IRISH
REPUBL

THE

PORTUGAL

SPAIN

ARCTIC
OCEAN

LAPLAND

NORWAY

FINLAND

RUSSIA

SWEDEN

ED KINGDOM

NORTH SEA

ESTONIA

BALTIC SEA

DENMARK

LATVIA

LITHUANIA

GREAT
RITAIN

HOLLAND

BELARUS

GERMANY

POLAND

BELGIUM

LUX.

UKRAINE

FRANCE

CZECH
REPUBLIC

CASPIAN SEA

SLOVAKIA

MOLDOVA

SWITZERLAND

AUSTRIA

HUNGARY

SLOVENIA

ROMANIA

BLACK SEA

CROATIA

YUGOSLAVIA

ITALY

BOSNIA
HERZEGOVINA

CORSICA

MONTENEGRO

BULGARIA

MACEDONIA

ALBANIA

SARDINIA

GREECE

MEDITERRANEAN SEA

SICILY

29

FRANCE

Guillaume is five years old. He lives in a house with his family: his father, mother, and his older sister, Camille.

In the evening, the whole family gets together for dinner. Their meal includes:

leek soup

veal scallop with cream and mushrooms

Camembert cheese and bread

a chocolate crepe

On Wednesday, Guillaume likes to go to the puppet show. It's extra special because Grandma Claudine takes him there.

On Sunday, they go to the market. There are a lot of things to buy. Guillaume carries the basket!

During the day, Guillaume goes to nursery school. The teacher's name is Isabelle. She often reads stories.

Guillaume and Camille have two months of summer vacation.
They visit Uncle Antoine. He lives in the country near a lake.

Can you find these on the big picture?

Uncle Antoine's house

the paraglider

the hikers

What kinds of things
do people do along
a lake?

GREAT BRITAIN

Every morning,
before going to school,
Cindy has breakfast.
She eats

scrambled eggs with
bacon

toast with orange
marmalade

a muffin

milk and cereals

fruit juice

*Do you eat the same
things for breakfast that
Cindy does?*

Look. The milkman came. There is a bottle of milk
in front of the house.
Cindy wears a uniform to school. She says hello to Mrs.
Lollypop, the crossing guard.

Today is Sunday and it's not raining. So Cindy's family has a picnic in the park. They spread a tablecloth on the ground. Everything they need is in a basket. The sandwiches taste great!

The British love sports. They invented rugby and soccer.

In the parks, people often play cricket. To play, they hit a ball with a wooden bat. They wear white uniforms.

On the river, you can see boat races. These are called shell races.

In the pubs, people often play darts.

SPAIN

Flamenco is a dance. Flamenco music is played with these instruments:

a guitar

a tambourine

The dancer herself plays castanets.

Make a fan! Take a sheet of paper and decorate it. Fold it like an accordion. Then fold it in half, gluing it in the middle.

34

Carmen is the girl in the green skirt. She is learning how to dance the flamenco. Her mother is watching while fanning herself.

Yanni lives on this island. There are many olive trees around his house. Today, Yanni came to the dock with his grandfather. They are sitting outside of a cafe.

GREECE

It's really hot here in the summer!

Thankfully, the houses are painted white. So it always stays cool inside.

Many of the people on the island are fishermen, like Yanni's father. He has a very colorful fishing boat. He fishes with a big net. The net needs to be fixed from time to time.

GERMANY

Ute is four years old. She lives in a nice house. Her parents, her brother Rudi, and her sister Kärstin live with her.

During the day Ute goes to preschool. She meets friends and plays games at preschool.

At Ute's house there are three garbage cans. One for paper, one for glass, and one for plastic!

It's Rudi's first day of school! He gets a paper horn filled with toys and candies.

Kärstin starts school at eight in the morning. But by one in the afternoon, she is done. Then she can play tennis.

Uncle Bernd and Ulrike are getting married. Before their wedding, they have a big party. It's the Polterabend. Their friends break white dishes to wish them luck.

At the fair, Stefie goes on the merry-go-round. She likes the wooden horses better than the Ferris wheel.

Stefie loves to visit her grandparents in Vienna. She goes to the cafe with them. Papi and Mamie drink coffee topped with whipped cream. All three eat tasty cakes.

Stefie lives with her family in a town. When she goes to parties, she wears a dirndl. A dirndl is a traditional costume.

Stefie likes to stop at bakeries and look inside. They are filled with cakes. Her favorites are

the Sachertorte

the Linzertorte

HUNGARY

On Easter day the boys spray the girls with perfume. The girls give painted eggs to the boys.

Would you like to color eggs?
Ask an adult to hard-boil the eggs in water. Add beets to the water if you want red eggs. Add chopped spinach leaves for green eggs. Then decorate them with paint.

The water in this pool comes from a hot spring. You can swim in it all year long. Some people even play chess in the pool.

Russian winters are very cold. There is a lot of snow.
People have to dress warmly. They can't wait to see the
sun again. So when spring comes, people pretend to
burn Father Winter!

RUSSIA

The Moscow circus is
well known. It has
wonderful acts.
Sometimes the show
is on ice.

Everyone skates, even
the bear!

The clowns do silly
things. They make the
children laugh.

The trapeze artist
jumps through the air.

REINDEER RACES IN LAPLAND

Jouni is a Laplander. He lives with his father, mother, and brother Yrjo. They live in a town of wooden houses in northern Europe. His family raises reindeer.

In summer, Yrjo and Jouni's dad leaves with the reindeer herd. He lives in a deer-skin tent.

In the winter, it is very cold. Everything is covered with snow. For two months it is dark all the time.

To celebrate the end of winter, a reindeer race is planned. Yrjo will race his favorite reindeer. He has hitched it to a long wooden sled. We hope he will win!

In winter, reindeer dig in the snow with their hoofs. They try to find plants to eat.

The Laplanders drink reindeer milk and eat reindeer meat. They like to suck on the bone marrow. They also like to eat dried reindeer tongue with coffee.

Laplanders make clothes with the reindeer skins. They make carpets and very warm blankets with the fur.

Look! Jouni's dad wears a funny hat with four points. It is the hat of the four winds. The rectangles on his belt show that he is married.

41

GOOD EUROPEAN DISHES

You can thank the Italians for inventing ice cream! In Italy, you can also eat great pizzas and all kinds of pasta.

spaghetti

farfalle

ziti

shells

fettucine

fusilli

Pasta can be eaten fresh. Italians like to eat their pasta cooked al dente. That means slightly crunchy.

What happens in Yanni's Greek town on Easter Sunday? A special meal is made. Lambs are roasted in open pits. When they are cooked, everyone eats together.

Carmen's family is eating paella. It is a Spanish meal. It is made with yellow rice, vegetables, meat, and seafood!

You are walking outside in Denmark and you get hungry. What do you do? You can stop for a smorebrod. It is a sandwich. It's made with fish, shrimp, or chicken.

Claudia is German. At night, her family eats a meal called the abendbrot. They eat cold cuts, cheese, and breads. There are all sorts of breads, like nut bread or onion bread.

Greek salad is really good! Here's how to make it:

slice 5 tomatoes and 1 onion

slice 1 cucumber and cut feta cheese in little cubes

in a salad bowl, make your dressing. Use olive oil, vinegar, salt, pepper, and oregano,

then add the olives, tomato, cucumber, feta, and onions. Mix it all up. It's ready!

SAINT LUCIA IN SWEDEN

In Sweden, they start getting ready for Christmas at the beginning of December.

A wreath is put on the dining room table. It has four candles. Every Sunday, a candle is lit.

The outside of the house is decorated. A pretty wreath is hung on the door. The feast starts on December 13 with Saint Lucia. It is the feast of light.

On Saint Lucia's day, people march holding candles. They also dress in special costumes.

For Saint Lucia, Ingrid, Lars, and Bjorn wake up their mom and dad with songs. Bjorn is dressed as a star. Ingrid is dressed as Saint Lucia. She brings coffee and cake to her parents.

It is December 25. Marie, Aurélien, and Axel are very happy. Santa Claus has come. And, under the tree, there are many gifts to open.

CHRISTMAS IN FRANCE

The Christmas tree is decorated with balls, garland, and stars.

One story says that Santa Claus comes from Lapland. He brings presents to children on a sled. The sled is pulled by reindeer.

On Christmas Eve, people eat a fancy meal. It is called the réveillon. There is a big cake shaped like a piece of wood. It is the Christmas log.

THE AMERICAS

Stewart

America is a very large continent. The arctic north is where Achouna the little Eskimo lives. It is quite different from José's hot Brazil! And what a shock it is to go from Stewart's skyscraper to an Amazonian Indian house!

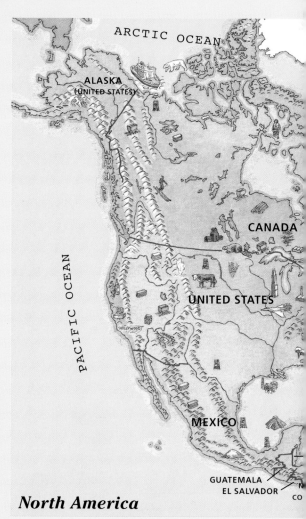

ARCTIC OCEAN

ALASKA
(UNITED STATES)

PACIFIC OCEAN

CANADA

UNITED STATES

HOLLYWOOD

MEXICO

GUATEMALA
EL SALVADOR
CO

North America

Achouna

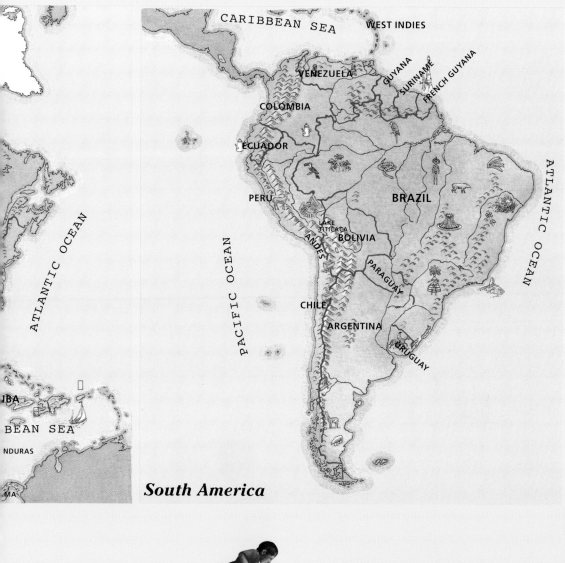

CARIBBEAN SEA   WEST INDIES

VENEZUELA   GUYANA SURINAME FRENCH GUYANA

COLOMBIA

ECUADOR

PERU

BRAZIL

ATLANTIC OCEAN

LAKE
TITICACA

ANDES   BOLIVIA

PACIFIC OCEAN

PARAGUAY

CHILE

ARGENTINA

URUGUAY

ATLANTIC OCEAN

IBA

BEAN SEA

NDURAS

MA

South America

José

47

THE UNITED STATES

Stewart is five years old. He lives with his family in a very, very tall building. This kind of building is called a skyscraper.

The yellow cars in the big picture are taxis. How many do you see?

On Halloween, Americans carve out pumpkins. They make holes for the eyes, nose, and mouth. Then they place a candle in the middle.

This is the city where Stewart lives. Everything is large: the buildings, the streets. Even some of the cars are big, like Cadillacs.

It's Halloween. Stewart and his friends dress up as ghosts, vampires, or other monsters. They go from house to house to get candy and other treats.

After school, Stewart plays basketball.
When he grows up, he wants to be a
professional basketball player.

Kevin, Stewart's brother, plays baseball
with his team. The whole family goes to
the game to root for him.

In the United States, people drive a lot. There are many highways. You can sit in your
car and buy food at a fast-food place or see a movie at a drive-in.

CANADA

How do you get the sap of out a sugar maple tree? You must make a hole in the tree. This is called tapping the tree. The sap is boiled down to make the maple syrup.

For breakfast, Conrad puts maple syrup on his pancakes.

Draw maple leaves on a piece of cardboard. Paint them in different colors. Then cut them out to make decorations.

Conrad goes hiking with his parents in a big pine forest. Loggers cut down trees. These trees will float down the river toward the mill.

**In Canada, winter is very cold. There is a lot of ice and snow.
That doesn't stop the Canadians from having fun.**

In Quebec, there is an ice sculpting contest during the carnival.

They have bed races on the cold streets of Ottawa.

Ice hockey is a lot of fun to play! It's the Canadians' favorite sport. Watch out for falls! You have to be protected. Remember to wear your helmet.

ESKIMOS

During the winter way up north, it is dark almost all the time. Children can't go out much. To keep busy they play cup-and-balls. They play this game with walrus bones.

To make a cup-and-ball you will need:

a toilet paper tube, a piece of string, a ball of newspaper.

The object of the game is to get the ball in the tube. Good luck!

This is Achouna's town. He is an Eskimo. He kisses his mom by rubbing his nose against hers. Achouna's dad is on his snowmobile. He is waiting for Achouna to go fishing.

Many animals live in the sea. Others live on the ice pack. This is the thick layer of ice that floats on the sea.

The polar bear's fur is very thick. So it doesn't feel the cold. The polar bear swims in the icy water.

The walrus digs at the bottom of the sea. It uses its two tusks to find food. It also uses them to get back on the bank. It sticks the tusks in the ice.

They dig a hole in the ice. Then they wait for the fish to bite. It is very cold! But they are bundled up. Achouna did not forget to wear his brand-new jacket.

MEXICO

Parents give their children a piñata for their birthday. They do this at Christmas time, too. A piñata is made out of cardboard. It is filled with candy and little presents.

The piñata is hung on a branch. Then a child is blindfolded. The child must hit the piñata with a stick to open it.

Have fun making a piñata. Use a cardboard box. Then decorate it and fill it with candy.

This is Juanita's and Carlos's town. Today is Juanita's birthday. She is five. Her brother is sucking on a sugar cane. He watches her bang on the piñata.

Tortillas can be filled with guacamole, a green avocado sauce.

Here's how to make guacamole:

With a fork, squash two ripe avocados to make a puree. Take 2 tomatoes, 1 onion, 1 green pepper, cut into small pieces, and mix them with the avocado puree. Add 2 tablespoons of olive oil, the juice of 1 lemon, and 1 tablespoon of cream. Add salt, pepper, and a pinch of coriander. The guacamole is ready. Put it in the refrigerator. Enjoy!

Men wear hats with large rims called sombreros. These hats protect them from the sun. People stay under the arcades to stay cool. They like to eat tortillas.

THE AMAZONIAN FOREST

High in the trees, howling monkeys let out screams. You can hear them from far away.

The colorful macaw also makes a lot of noise. And it uses its beak as a nut cracker.

The great anteater walks on the ground. It eats ants and termites. It uses its sticky tongue to grab them.

The Amazonian forest is the biggest forest in the world. The high trees grow very close to each other. This blocks out the sun. On the ground it is almost dark even in the daytime.

Indian people live in the Amazonian forest. It is hot and humid, and often rains heavily.

These people all live all together in big open houses. They sleep in hammocks.

Some people fish with arrows. Others hunt with a blowgun. A blowgun is a long hollow tube. The Indians put a little poisoned arrow in it. Then they blow through the tube. This sends the arrow at their prey.

BRAZIL

Here is how to dress up as a carnival dancer:

Make a long skirt with crepe paper. Decorate it with glitter and stickers.

Gather the top of the skirt with colorful ribbons.

Wear a bright colored bathing suit. Slip on the skirt. Put a scrunchie on each arm. Wrap a scarf around your head. Put on some jewelry and party makeup. You are ready for the parade.

In Rio de Janeiro, there is a carnival once a year. It lasts for a week. People come to this carnival from around the world. There is a parade of floats, musicians, and dancers. The dancers spend a year making their costumes.

José lives just above the very beautiful Ipanema beach. He lives in a favela. A favela is a group of houses with no bathroom. It is built with corrugated iron and wood. Very poor people live in them.

José is six years old. He has four brothers and two sisters. His parents do not have much money. To help them, José has to work. He sells fritters on Ipanema beach.

His friend Antonio sells newspapers in the center of Rio.

Like all Brazilians, José and Antonio love soccer. Whenever they have free time, they play ball with their friends.

THE ANDES

Pablo is Indian. He lives with his family. They live on the edge of Lake Titicaca, in the Andes. The Andes is a very long mountain chain.

Plants called totoras grow on the edge of the lake. People use totoras to make many things:

boats

house roofs

mats

Flute and tambourine music is very lively. It makes you feel like moving. Pablo grabs his friend Celia for a dance. She keeps her bowler hat on and twirls her layered skirts.

Llamas are very strong. But watch out! Don't anger them or they will spit at you.

Pablo's mother dyes llama wool. Then she weaves it to make hats and ponchos.

Pablo's mother makes lunch. She cooks llama meat that has been dried in the sun.

Many people crowd into the truck to go to town.

It's market day. Women sit on the ground and sell their goods.

AFRICA

Africa is very hot.
Join Manda, the little Touareg.
He lives in a tent in the desert.
Take a walk in the market
of a big city. Discover the town where
Yassama and her family live.
Also meet

SENEGAL
GAMBIA
GUINEA-BISSAU
GUI
SIERRA LE

Aboubakar

Aminata

Ahmed

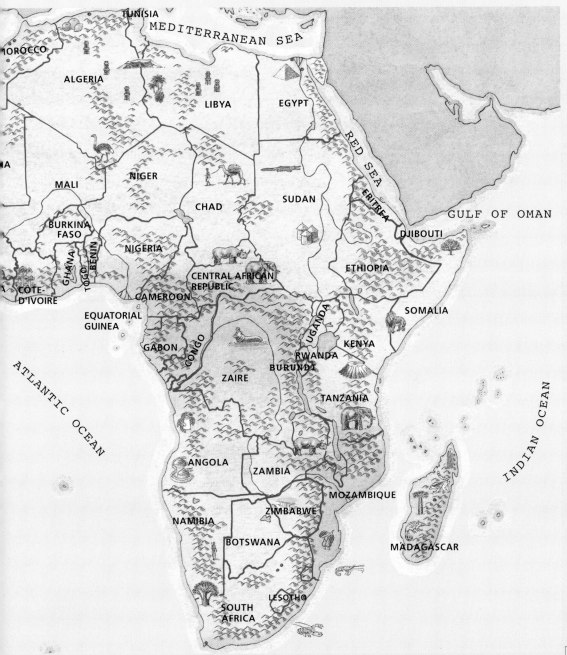

MEDITERRANEAN SEA

TUNISIA

MOROCCO

ALGERIA

LIBYA

EGYPT

RED SEA

GULF OF OMAN

MALI

NIGER

CHAD

SUDAN

ERITREA

DJIBOUTI

BURKINA FASO

NIGERIA

CENTRAL AFRICAN REPUBLIC

ETHIOPIA

GHANA

TOGO

BENIN

COTE D'IVOIRE

CAMEROON

EQUATORIAL GUINEA

GABON

CONGO

ZAIRE

UGANDA

RWANDA

BURUNDI

KENYA

SOMALIA

TANZANIA

ATLANTIC OCEAN

ANGOLA

ZAMBIA

MOZAMBIQUE

NAMIBIA

ZIMBABWE

BOTSWANA

MADAGASCAR

INDIAN OCEAN

SOUTH AFRICA

LESOTHO

63

NORTH AFRICA

In their booths, or souks, the craftsmen make different things.

Sitting at his wheel, the potter makes a clay pot.

Tanners soak pieces of leather in these dye tubs. They dye the pieces different colors.

The leather worker makes purses or wallets with the dyed leather.

Ahmed loves to walk in the market. He is walking with his grandmother Yamina. Ahmed holds on tight to her hand. He does not want to get lost.

The women made a lot of food for the wedding. They made

bread

couscous with seminola wheat, vegetables, lamb, and merguez

very sweet cakes with honey, almonds, and orange blossom

tea with mint that is drunk very hot and very sweet

It's Aunt Zohra's wedding. The party is going to last several days. Women belly dance. They yell with shrieking calls. These calls roll in the throat and are called youyous.

THE TOUAREG CAMP

Touareg men wrap long scarves around their faces. This protects them from the sun and the sand winds. These scarves are sometimes blue. The blue dye rubs off on the Touaregs' faces. That is why they are called the blue men.

Find these things in the big picture:

the water skin that keeps the water cool

the camel's saddle

Manda is a Touareg. He lives with his family. They live under a skin tent in the Sahara Desert. During the day it is very hot. At night it is very cold.

The camel has three stomachs. They hold a lot of water. And its hump holds fat that feeds the camel. The hump goes down as the fat is used. The camel can walk for a long time without eating or drinking.

To stand up, the camel unfolds its back legs first. The rider better hold on tight.

Sometimes, they take the tent down. Then they travel with the camels in a group called a caravan. They go to find food for the goat herd. Touaregs who move all the time are nomads.

A CITY IN AFRICA

In western Africa, women buy these things at the market:

Bowls and cups. These are made from the shells of dried fruit.

Squares of cloth in many designs and colors. The women make boubous with these. Boubous are long and large tunics. They help to keep people cool in the hot sun.

Big markets are found in African towns. People come from far away to sell their goods. Other people come to buy what they need. Yassama arrives from her town with her father. It's the first time that she has taken the bush-taxi.

In the city, some people work in offices. Others do their work in the street:

the man who sells toys

the shoe shiner

the windshield washer

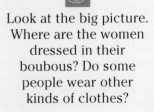

Look at the big picture. Where are the women dressed in their boubous? Do some people wear other kinds of clothes?

It's very noisy. Everyone is talking and laughing. Yassama finds that the town is very big. She is a little scared of crossing the street. There are so many cars. So she holds on to her dad's hand.

FARMING

In certain parts of Africa, people grow millet. It's a cereal like wheat.

Millet grains are kept in attics. The attics are built on stands that are like little feet. Being up high keeps the grain safe. If it was on the ground, field mice could eat it. Or it could get wet from the rain.

Women grind the millet. They use tools carved from a tree trunk. That is how they make millet flour.

Before planting the seeds, the earth must be plowed. To plow means to turn over. Here men plow with a hoe called the daba. It's hard work. They sing to help them keep going.

This is along the seashore in Mauritania. Fishermen catch fish called mullets. Dolphins help them in their work.

It is hard to fish this way.

One man checks underwater. When he sees a group of fish, he tells his fellow workers. A group of fish is called a school of fish.

They throw their nets into the sea. Then they hit the top of the water with sticks.

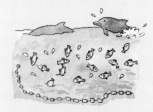

The dolphins hear the noise and come close to the nets. Without knowing it, the dolphins push the fish into the nets.

THE TOWN

The houses are grouped together. They are circled by a fence. All of the members of a family live together and form a clan. A clan is made up of children, parents, aunts, uncles, cousins, and grandparents.

The walls of the houses are made with clay. The clay is made from dirt mixed with straw. The roof is covered with dried millet stalks.

Yassama lives with her family in a town in Mali. She is part of the Dogon people. She helps her mother make pottery. She also has to watch Domo, her little brother. Domo is always getting into trouble.

Yassama and the other women prepare the meal. They serve everyone else. Then the women rest in front of the house. That is when they eat their millet food. The food is called gruel. They eat with their fingers.

MEALS

Millet gruel can be seasoned with a green sauce. This sauce is made from the leaves of the baobab tree. Sometimes vegetables, such as onions, are added.

Millet is also used to make flat cakes and beer.

There is not much meat. So it is only eaten on special occasions. Sometimes dried fish is bought at the market.

THE TOWN FEAST

In Africa, music is used in every part of life. Whether happy or sad, people use music. There are many musical instruments.

A drum.
The player wears it around the neck.

The balaphon. This is a row of wooden slats on top of dried fruit shells.

The kora. This is also called the African harp. It is made with half of a dried fruit shell.

Today is the feast to honor the dead. Masked dancers move to the beat of the music. Yassama watches the dancers. She likes the masks. But she cannot know the person behind the mask!

Ears and eyes wide open, Yassama listens to the griot. He is telling an animal story. The little children are sometimes scared. They wonder if the lion is going to eat the gazelle.

THE GRIOT

The griot is a poet and storyteller. He knows the past of the towns and the families. He plays a small drum when he tells his stories. The drum is called a tama.

The griot doesn't write down his stories. All of the tales he tells are in his mind. When a griot dies, it is as if a library has disappeared. Some people want to honor a griot when he dies. So they place him into a baobab trunk.

EVERYDAY LIFE

Babies are taken care of with a lot of love. They are fed anytime they are hungry. And they never leave their mothers. Their mothers carry them on their backs.

Not all towns have schools. But each school has a lot of children in each class. Every day, Aminata has a long way to walk. Her school is very far from her house.

African children love to play this simple game. It's called dosu.

Take a stone and bury it in the sand. Make a little pile above it. Then make as many sand piles as there are players.

Call your friends. Each chooses a sand pile. The winner is the one who finds the stone. Then the winner buries the stone and the game starts again.

To have fun, children play with whatever they can find. Their families do not have enough money to buy toys. So the children make their own toys. Aboubakar made these nice little cars with wire.

EVERYDAY LIFE

Children can't play all day. They must also help their parents with the daily chores.

Aminata is the oldest one in her family. She has many brothers and sisters. She has to help her mother take care of them.

She washes her little brother in the tub.

She braids her sister Fatoumata's hair.

Aminata gets water at the well. She brings it back in a bowl.

Aminata also learns how to take care of the house. She does the cooking and the wash with her mother.

Her brother, Aboubakar, is in charge of the goat herd.

Some towns do not have doctors. So medical teams come from time to time.
They give shots to the children. This helps to keep them from getting sick.

When the children are sick, Aminata's mother sometimes takes them to the healer.
He uses magic, herbs, and dances to heal them.

OCEANIA

Oceania is made up of many islands. The biggest one is Australia. Visit Pamela's ranch. Discover strange animals such as the kangaroo. Meet Australian Aborigines. Leave with Luc the Polynesian in a canoe.

INDIAN OCEAN

MARIANA
ISLANDS

HAWAII
(USA)

FEDERATED STATES
OF MICRONESIA

PACIFIC

OCEAN

PAPUA
NEW GUINEA

POLYNESIA

CORAL SEA

NEW
CALEDONIA

FRENCH
POLYNESIA
TAHITI

AUSTRALIA

NEW
ZEALAND

TASMAN SEA

AN AUSTRALIAN CITY

Australians like sports very much. They mostly like water sports such as

surfing

windsurfing

The sea is sometimes dangerous. It has big waves and sharks. Thankfully, lifeguard teams are there to help people in danger.

Paul is five years old. He lives in a big modern seaside city called Sydney. He sails with his father. He likes that very much!

Pamela lives on a ranch. It's a big farm where they raise
cows and sheep. They herd the cows with cars and
motorcycles. Sometimes they even use helicopters.

ON A RANCH

There is no town near
the ranch. There is not
even another house
nearby. Pamela can't
go to school because
it is too far.

She takes classes by
using a two-way radio.
She does this with
other children who live
on ranches.

She can ask questions
and the school teacher
answers.

ABORIGINES

Aborigines paint on bark. They use only four colors. The red and the brown of the earth. The white of chalk. And the black of charcoal.

Aborigines invented the boomerang. It is a piece of wood with a bend in it. When someone throws it, it comes back to the thrower. They use it to hunt birds. Today, people around the world play with boomerangs.

Aborigines were the first people to live in Australia. Some of them still live in the desert. They hunt and dance to music. The music is played on a long bamboo tube. Aborigines call this the didjeridu. Other Aborigines have left the desert and live in town.

In Australia, there are animals that don't live any place else.

The kangaroo carries its young in a pocket on the tummy.

The dingo is a wild desert dog. It sometimes attacks sheep.

The skink is a big lizard. It sticks out its blue tongue when it is scared.

The flying squirrel glides from one tree to the next.

The mother koala eats eucalyptus leaves. Her baby is on her back.

The song of the kookaburra sounds like a big laugh.

NEW ZEALAND

This is the street where Tony lives. He lives in a house with his parents and his brothers. Tony is in front of his house. He's going to ride his bike.

In the park, Tony and two of his friends play rugby. The ball is oval. Like most New Zealanders, Tony likes that sport. His father will soon take him to a rugby match.

In the summer, Tony's family takes long walks in the mountains. Everything is green. Only the sheep herds make large white patches.

Tony likes to look at the geysers. Geysers are big water jets. They shoot out of the ground suddenly.

Tony presses his nose against the nose of Kupe. Kupe is his Maori friend. That's how the Maoris say hello to each other. The Maoris were the first people to live in New Zealand. Kupe's father is making a beautiful mask.

A POLYNESIAN ISLAND

The coconut trees have rings on their trunks. This stops the rats from eating the coconuts.

With the leaves and the bark of the coconut tree, women weave

balls for the children

baskets

You can make a funny mask. Use half of a coconut shell, wool, wire, and shells.

On the sandy beach, Jeannette plays with a giant clam. Her cousins climb up the coconut trees to pick coconuts. They will eat them and drink the coconut milk.

Jeannette's father goes in the water. It is warm and clear. You can see the bottom! He is going out to fish with Luc, Jeannette's big brother. They will fish in his wooden canoe.

Beautiful flowers grow on this island, flowers such as

the tiare

the hibiscus

the frangipani

These flowers are used to make crowns. The crowns are given to guests to welcome them.

Sometimes a girl wears a tiare on her right ear. This means that she has a boyfriend. But sometimes it is on the left ear. This means that the girl is looking for a boyfriend.

GAMES FROM AROUND THE WORLD

Return each toy to its owner.

Juanita the Mexican

Kosuke the Japanese

Aboubakar the African

the metal toy

the piñata

the kite

Aboubakar, the African, plays with the metal toy. Kosuke, the Japanese, plays with the kite. Juanita, the Mexican, plays with the piñata

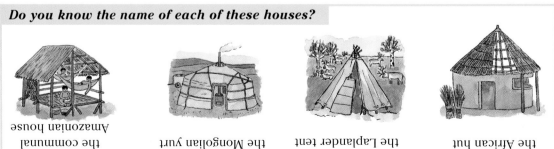

Do you know the name of each of these houses?

the communal Amazonian house

the Mongolian yurt

the Laplander tent

the African hut

Do you know where these animals live?

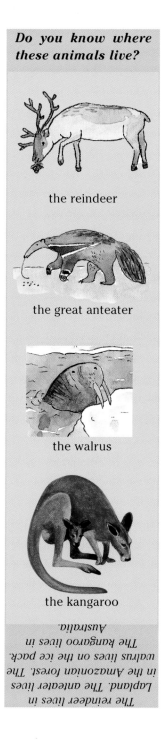

the reindeer

the great anteater

the walrus

the kangaroo

The reindeer lives in Lapland. The anteater lives in the Amazonian forest. The walrus lives on the ice pack. The kangaroo lives in Australia.

Look at these musical instruments. Which ones do not come from Africa?

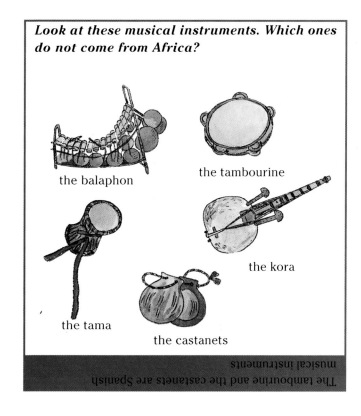

the balaphon

the tambourine

the tama

the kora

the castanets

The tambourine and the castanets are Spanish musical instruments.

Here are a lot of good things to eat and drink. What is the name of each of these dishes? Where do they come from?

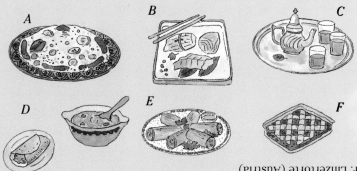

A

B

C

D

E

F

A. Couscous (North Africa). B. Raw fish (Japan). C. Tea with mint (North Africa). D. Tortillas with guacamole (Mexico) E. Nems (China) F. Linzertorte (Austria)

INDEX

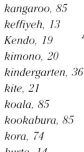